AF654697

Flower The Way for Peace

"You can develop the right attitude toward others if you have kindness, love and respect for them, and a clear realization of the oneness of all human beings."

- His Holiness the Dalai Lama

Dr. Vidyasagar Abburi

BlueRose ONE.com
Stories Matter
NewDelhi • London

BLUEROSE PUBLISHERS
India | U.K.

BlueRose ONE.com
Stories Matter
NewDelhi • London

For permissions, requests or inquiries regarding this publication, please contact:

BLUEROSE PUBLISHERS
www.BlueRoseONE.com
info@bluerosepublishers.com
+91 8882 898 898
+4407342408967

ISBN: 978-93-7018-401-5

First Edition: April 2025

Contents

This book is dedicated to my parents who are a source of inspiration to pursue goals that leave the world a better place to live than what we inherited.

I am thankful to Mr. Ramesh Kosaraju for helping me with editing.

Chapter One

Introduction

"If we could see the miracle of a single flower clearly our whole life would change."

- Buddha

We all aspire to be happy and at peace. Some of us may even agree that the purpose of life itself is to be happy and share happiness with everyone around us. Yet, such a state of mind is evasive, fleeting, and unsustainable. In human history, the best of minds have sought the magic formula for sustainable peace, harmony, and happiness in our lives.

If happiness is the absence of suffering, pursuit of knowledge and wisdom to identify the root causes of suffering and finding the way to be free from those causes is enlightening. Philosophers and scientists have dedicated their lives to the study of human psychology, physiology, and neurosciences to find the elusive elixir for the well-being, peace and happiness of all. The mystics, religious scholars, and noble saints too shared pearls of wisdom to guide humanity, for harmony, love, and goodwill.... among all.

In the history of evolving humans, dispersed in big expanse of lands all over the world and flowing through the twirls of times, many schools of thought have evolved. Though each is unique, all of them have a common thread of oneness of all life with love, compassion, and goodwill for all. They are all ways to open our minds to the light of wisdom and to dispel darkness arising out of our inability to see things as they are. The practices they suggested, such as mindfulness, are to help us become free from defilements of a conditioned mind and awaken us to the truth of oneness.

"If with a pure mind a person speaks or acts, happiness follows him like his never-departing shadow." - Buddha

The key message from all religions, philosophies, and scientific findings is that everything in the universe is so intricately entangled and connected that we are a microcosm of the universe itself.

Suffering could be physical due to pains, disease, or old age, maybe mental due to the loss of loved ones, emotional trauma, or dissatisfaction over non-fulfilment of desires or aspirations. However, at the bottom of most suffering lies the defilements of mind such as anger, hatred, jealousy, and ill will.

It was very difficult for me to be free from disturbing defilements of mind such as cravings and aversions; despite being driven by an altruistic purpose of working for the common good and well-being of all. After prolonged self-introspection, I realized that self-centeredness, ego, attachment to everything associated with self like self-image, beliefs, ideas, opinions are possible causes. Then, the biggest challenge was to find ways to become free from the ever recurring elusive 'enormity of I'.

Lives of great persons inspire and remind us, that we too can experience the light within, sublime our lives for the benefit of many in harmony with nature and its beings. I tried to read and fathom the teachings of Ramana Maharshi, Swami Vivekananda, Paramahansa Yogananda, Swami Ranganathananda, Western thinkers, philosophers and veritable *Upanishads* and the sacred *Bhagavad Gita*.

"A generous heart, kind speech, and a life of service and compassion are the things which renew humanity." - Buddha

"Change yourself and you have done your part in changing the world." - Paramahansa Yogananda

As an involuntary consequence, I started exploring meditation techniques too. Despite all efforts, the traces of defilements in my mind haunt me and the only solace is that I was aware of their presence. So, I continued looking for direction and guidance for the way forward.

One school of thought which has stood the test of time, for more than 2,500 years and is still revered by many, is taught by Siddharth Gautama (500 BC), known as the Buddha, meaning 'the Enlightened One'. It is endorsed and practiced by millions even now. Gautama encouraged monks, nuns, and common householders to practice the 'noble eightfold path' to be free from suffering and to develop love, compassion and goodwill for all. It has been accepted and found useful by people from all walks of life including common people, kings and queens, religious people, monks, householders, and intellectuals across the world because it is simple, scientific, universal, and effective.

Meditation is an integral part of any spiritual or religious system. *Vipassana*, a meditation technique taught by Buddha as an integral part of the noble eightfold path, has been practiced and passed on to many generations in Myanmar. Now it is available from the teachings of Sri Satyanarayana Goenka fondly called *Guruji* with love, respect, and gratitude. For those in search of peace, practicing meditation as taught by him is worth exploring.

"Happiness comes when your work and words are of benefit to others." - Buddha

I would like to submit that my views presented in this book are purely based on personal understanding and do not represent the teachings of Sri Satyanarayana Goenkaji. Any inquisitive student can get more information on *Vipassana* through literature, videos, and *Vipassana* meditation centers all over the world, where they teach how to practice.

I first tried *Vipassana* meditation by joining a 10-day course in the year 2000. It was incidental and special in a way. I was diagnosed with a spinal injury, suffering from prolapsed, degenerated discs. I was even advised of surgery by specialist doctors. The immediate motive for joining the course was to possibly find relief from the pain and to face any consequences. As a pleasant surprise, after completing the course I walked out free from pain and till now no surgical intervention has been needed and I continue to be active. I am aware that *Vipassana* is not meant for this, but it's difficult to speculate on the possible by-products!

The purpose of *Vipassana* is to understand the way out of all kinds of suffering and realize true freedom; freedom from one's own conditioned reactive mind with defilements arising out of delusion, unbounded cravings, and aversions. Most significantly, freedom from bondages and attachment of the perceived "I", me and mine. I faced several challenges while trying to walk the path of *Dhamma*, the noble eightfold path. As a householder, I had to play the role of a family man and as a professional I had to earn a livelihood. These roles

---

put me in varied situations that result in attachment, based on social context and norms of the society at large. I could not remain detached, and I continued to react to situations, though the path required me to be responsive and not reactive.

Slowly, I realized that the ones walking this path all along need mindful practice, patience, endurance, and equanimity. There are no shortcuts; practice is the key. With the support from teachers, family members, and other practitioners, I could continue the journey.

During the years of tough treading, I started liking the pursuit of *Dhamma*. Hopefully, I may not look back as it is not about 'me' anymore in my 'thoughts and actions'. Overall, it has been a rewarding pursuit. The conscious aspiration holds me to mindful empathy, love, and compassion for all.

The main idea behind this book is to share thoughts on reasons for conflict and wars which cause immense suffering to millions at different levels. It is also to gain insight on how a noble eightfold path as taught by Gautama Buddha can be a way forward for global peace and harmony. If not a panacea, it can soothe wounds and change the world for the better.

Wars are driven by fear, greed, blind faith, and a wrong understanding of the basic tenets of any form of religion. Wars have been fought because of the notion that 'we' are different from 'them', or that 'our way' is superior to 'their way' - whether those others are neighboring cities, states, distant nations, or indigenous populations.

"The root of suffering is attachment." - Buddha

"One who acts on truth is happy in this world and beyond."
- Buddha

Wars outside are a reflection of the prejudices and internal conflict between positive and negative thoughts arising out of attachment to the individual self. If most of the individual minds can be pure and free from afflictions of hatred and ill will, the possibility of wars will decrease significantly. Feeling and experiencing oneness of all beings and acting with love, compassion, and respect can only be the true path to peace.

Strength, power, or military might cannot dispel darkness. It is light and light alone that can do so. We will be able to bring light by purifying our minds - the light which shines bright with love, compassion, and goodwill for all.

Listening to stories interest me and even more so if they are about Buddha. I liked the one often mentioned in Zen Buddhism where Buddha gives a silent sermon by holding up a flower. The wise disciple Mahakashyap acknowledges it with a smile and bows to the flower. The story is considered important as it is an example of the direct transmission of wisdom without using words. Buddha opts to convey the ineffable nature of wisdom in silence; an allegory seeking to delve into the flower's way of life, for deeper insight into the 'Truths in Nature', and the ways of human life.

In the last two millennia, the instances of patches of human cultures living in harmony existed inspired by wise men like Buddha. In the last 100 years, the relevance of the

---

"The best way to be happy is to strive to make others happy."
- Swamy Ranganathananda

teachings of Buddha has increased manifold. Socially, most people are driven by the need for inner joy, to be closer to their true nature. All indications point towards reformative changes in the history of humans for peaceful, harmonious coexistence.

The need is a 'free mind' - free from cravings, aversions and delusion, free from jealousy and ill will. The need is for hearts and minds radiating love and peace blissfully. The way to develop the qualities of love and kindness is to walk the time tested noble eightfold path. With the advent of great scientific discoveries, while understanding the ways of nature and its universal laws, the scientists of Quantum Physics have endorsed the truth of ancient wisdom.

In this book I have presented 'Flower's Way of Life' as an echo for 'Oneness of Life' which is also symbolic of the cycle of life, unity of life, cosmic order, and interconnection of everything. The life of the flower itself represents all the noble qualities and virtues that we seek to develop. Eventually, it reflects the goal of spiritual awakening and enlightenment. The noble eightfold path of Buddha is a way to cultivate noble qualities of loving kindness, altruistic joy, compassion, and equanimity. I am an optimist - earnest and hopeful that these shared thoughts will be helpful to householders who are looking for peace and harmony in this very life.

"Believe nothing, no matter where you read it, or who said it, no matter if I have said it, unless it agrees with your own reason and your own common sense." - Buddha

It is very important to note here that Buddha's teachings are methods to experience reality and not reality itself, just as finger-pointing at the moon is not the moon itself. His teachings are a means of practice, not something to hold on to as a belief or to worship. His teaching is like a raft to cross the river and reach the shore of liberation.

He emphasized that experiential wisdom is the only way to liberate yourself from bondage and suffering. Finally, the result might be perfection in the manifestation and expression of humility and gratitude - in our speech, thoughts, and actions. In the following chapters, we will explore how ancient wisdom, modern insights, and nature itself guide us toward lasting peace, harmony, and happiness.

"If you are depressed you are living in the past if you are anxious you are living in the future, if you are at peace, you are living in the present." - Lao Tzu

Chapter Two

In Quest of Peace

"The secret of health for both mind and body is not to mourn for the past, nor to worry about the future, but to live the present moment wisely and earnestly."

- Buddha

The vision of a pure and free world, where hearts suffuse with love and kindness, may sound dreamy and even Utopian. But is it not what the world needs and even deserves? A world wherein everyone abides by joy, empathy, awareness, and understanding. Don't we need to avert the wars in the future for a secure, peaceful, and safe living?

We can work for a world where the present and future generations will be safe, secure, and peaceful without being threatened by insanity of wars. Together, we can share positive and peaceful thoughts and actions to heal the disturbed collective consciousness. The path to this starts with transformation at an individual level to purify the mind - free from ego, greed, hatred & ill will - and experience love, compassion, and sympathetic joy.

Evolution and Progress:

We, humans as a species, have come a long way in terms of progress. Life was very difficult for almost everyone in the history of humankind on this planet Earth but for the progress made since the scientific revolution started in the 16th century. In the annals of human history, this period is marked as a major transition, a decisive change for modern times, for hope and scientific achievements.

People had to work hard in fields and yet vulnerable to famine. There were no medicines for handling pain, infections, inflammation, airborne/waterborne communicable

---

"Peace begins within yourself." - Buddha

"When you arise in the morning, think of what a precious privilege it is to be alive - to breathe, to think, to enjoy, to love."
- Marcus Aurelius

diseases and people died in millions for want of health care solutions. We have been very successful in the exploration of truth and through great scientific discoveries and inventions, we could improve the quality of life to an incredible level of comfort and control over the vagaries of nature.

The human mind with intellect, logic, and reason deducted the infinite universe and the ways of nature with surety. Belief gave way to knowledge, paving the way for advances in science and technology.

Logic and rational thinking, reason, and critical thinking have been the basis for advances in science and technology. We could learn the laws and ways of nature to an extent that it makes the infinite universe and our place in that comprehensible. We also mastered the art of drawing immense benefits from nature itself for survival and growth.

Throughout history, innovation has reshaped how we live, heal, and connect. The printing press transformed the way knowledge was, just as the internet does today. Advancements in medicine, from vaccinations to modern gene therapy, have continuously extended life.

From the invention of the wheel to the first spaceflight, each breakthrough has changed not only how we move through the world but also how we see it. The wheels of the cart evolved to become space flights; the abacus into the computer; the computing to the Artificial Intelligence. The vaccinations became gene therapy; the scalpels turned into robotic arms.

"I have been impressed with the urgency of doing. Knowing is not enough; we must apply. Being willing is not enough; we must do."
- Leonardo da Vinci

Medicines were discovered to save millions from diseases and eventual deaths. Agriculture and farming became scientific for plenty of food, even amidst the famines and the floods. Science turned the hardships into bearable comforts. The order in the nature was respected and understood; its vagaries were tamed.

Yet, the tragedy of the truth of humans remains; it is the persistent enigma of how to cultivate peace in ourselves and in the world around us. How can the multitude of individual soul's influence and shape collective wisdom? But why these apparent limitations? Many hints exist but it is often complicated.

We created a language of concepts, symbols, and words to share and communicate ideas. These very words, ideas, and abstractions acquired an appearance of reality, and our minds became prisoners of their own creation. We started living in a world of symbolic words, concepts and abstractions away from reality. These symbolic words and concepts created divisions and barriers based on religions, communities, regions, and nations. These divisions and negative qualities like craving for power and domination, fear, and insecurity caused conflicts and wars.

We remain very vulnerable to the immeasurable loss and misery that we are capable of inflicting on ourselves due to wars. The important requirement for our survival as well as evolution is global peace and living in harmony with nature.

"It had long since come to my attention that people of accomplishment rarely sat back and let things happen to them. They went out and happened to things." - Leonardo da Vinci

Societal conflict:

Throughout history, people have been shaped by the information they consume - whether through oral traditions, religious teachings, political ideologies, or digital content, the cycle of influence remains the same. They created abstract symbols for social identity as a group to enrich their lives as social beings. The symbols evolved in society to help improve the quality of life. The nation, the community and the religion are examples of such abstract human constructs which served as frameworks for social cohesion.

Such concepts were helpful for organizing human societies and creating frameworks through which we navigate the complexities of life. But they are not physical, natural things that exist in the universe. They are mental constructs and ideas we have developed over time to manage collective identity, culture, resources, and beliefs.

A nation is often defined by geographical boundaries, languages, laws, and shared history. All these are creations meant for convenience, security, sovereignty, and so on. But these boundaries are artificial, often drawn arbitrarily and possess no inherent existence in nature.

The idea of a nation was the creation of humans which is good to an extent that it gives citizens independence, a sense of identity, shared dreams, and belongingness. It becomes dysfunctional when we fail to see that our nation's progress depends on the well-being and prosperity of all the nations

---

"Nothing in life is to be feared; it is only to be understood."
- Marie Curie

"When the power of love overcomes the love of power the world will know peace." - Jimi Hendrix

on our planet. Unfortunately, many wars are fought under the premise of nation and the associated exulted emotional perceptions of reality.

Religion is a framework created by humans to make sense of the unknown, to explain existence, and to guide moral behavior. They are ideas and practices passed down through generations, helping people relate to the divine, to each other and to the world around them, providing deep meaning and connection. Religion nurtured the cultures and infused moral and ethical cores, a positive contribution.

Religions should help us become better human beings with love, compassion, goodwill and free us from hatred and ill will. Since religions develop strong emotive affiliations, they have been a major cause of conflicts and even wars. Religions failed many times to prevent us from being inhuman to the extent of harming and causing suffering to millions due to wars based on religion. This happened as many of us gave importance to rites and rituals forgetting the essential message of love and oneness which is common among all religions.

Further, individuals born into poverty often face insurmountable barriers in escaping it due to a lack of access to education, healthcare, or employment opportunities and therefore poverty perpetuates itself across generations. Systemic neglect of the poor and disregard for their humanity stems from the belief that some individuals or groups are more deserving of wealth and resources than

---

"Loneliness and the feeling of being unwanted is the most terrible poverty." - Mother Teresa

others. The most important factor is the lack of social mobility and access to opportunities for those who are born into poverty.

Inequality is unsustainable because it leads to social unrest, deteriorating human development, and weakened societal cohesion. In a world where resources and opportunities are unevenly distributed, systemic disparities perpetuate cycles of poverty and lack of development.

Poverty is not just about the absence of money, but the absence of opportunity, healthcare, education, and safety. Efforts such as the Sustainable Development Goals (SDGs) by the UN which aim to end poverty and reduce inequality, are steps in the right direction. Divisive social constructs, poverty and inequalities, unbridled cravings, and aversions lead to conflict and wars.

The diversity of the world can sometimes be a source of conflict when it is seen as a threat rather than a celebration of the richness of life. The diversity in cultures, languages, and religions may become undercurrents for conflicts. They may try to impose their own beliefs or values on others, leading to violence or persecution. The solution lies in the evolutionary realization of humane values. However, true transformation will come only when we realize that all people, regardless of nationality, are connected through shared humanity and destiny. We also should realize that individual well-being depends on the well-being of all.

"Poverty is the worst form of violence." - Mahatma Gandhi

Personal inner conflict:

The human paradox is that though endowed with extraordinary abilities to discover oneself and their place in the cosmos in search of truth, we find it difficult to conduct ourselves with enlightened self-interest. We fail to see that the well-being of an individual/community/nation depends on the well-being of all at the global level and the ecosystem we live in. We find it difficult to lead lives in harmony with nature in peaceful coexistence.

The systemic maladies are due to the combined, integrated manifestations of personal defilements. So, handling of the personal inner conflicts is vital. The only way out of this is to purify our minds and become free from defilements in the subconscious minds.

We humans are blessed with metacognition, the ability to think about how we think, self-awareness, and a higher level of consciousness. But unfortunately, we also have become victims of the workings of our own mind. Though at a conscious level we try to be logical, rational, and objective to pursue and enhance the quality of life, we are controlled mostly by our subconscious mind which operates in auto mode.

Our subconscious mind guides our behavior moment by moment. It's like a hidden algorithm responding automatically to life's inputs. Often, we don't even realize these automatic responses shape our thoughts and actions.

"Our life is what our thoughts make it." - Marcus Aurelius

U.S. corpsman carrying an injured child away from the battle in Hué, Vietnam 1968

"Kindness should become the natural way of life, not the exception."
- Buddha

The subconscious mind is like a hidden program running quietly in the background, guiding our reactions unless we consciously notice it.

The sensory feelings of pleasant and unpleasant experiences fashion inner aversions, and cravings - initially in bits but later they turn into involuntary diffused habits. Eventually, sages like Buddha warn, they become overwhelming factors for our behavior and attitudes. Buddha warns that the root cause of all suffering is due to cravings and aversions. Cravings magnify as greed, passion, and self-centered nature; even may end up as fear and anxiety. Compulsive desire of clinging to wealth, power, and material possessions, can drive individuals and entire societies toward greed and exploitation, often at the expense of others.

Aversion is a mental state characterized by hatred, fear, and resentment toward others. The aversions manifest as conceit, anger, hatred, ill will and jealousy. Aversion is often the result of fear of the unknown or fear of losing control and whether that fear is directed at other nations, groups, or individuals. It is this aversion that leads to war, violence, and discrimination.

When people fear the other due to differences in race, religion, or ideology, they are more likely to view these differences as a threat and take violent action. The hostility fueled by aversion has been the cause of countless wars and genocides throughout history.

"Look well into thyself; there is a source of strength which will always spring up if thou wilt always look." - Marcus Aurelius

We need to free our subconscious mind from the defilements of preconditioned response, which Buddha calls mental formations. The volitional predisposition of our mind should be free from negative qualities such as anger, hatred, ill will, jealousy, conceit, and ego-centered arrogance. A mind free from these impurities, naturally emanates love, compassion, and goodwill for all.

Reactive behavior in isolation or in groups, including wars at the national levels, depend on the status of individual subconscious diffusions. Buddha's focus as a solution was to free the individual minds of aversions and cravings. Buddha shared his wisdom through the noble eightfold path which is a path for purification of mind.

The Predicament of Wars:

Human knowledge has expanded exponentially; but the wisdom to avoid wars and conflicts is a distant dream. The common man is misguided in justifying the reasons for conflict. The reasons could be misplaced convictions or beliefs and leaders driven by greed for power, control, and domination. The essential root cause is a lack of connection with fellow human beings, and nature at large. These disconnects breed fear, distrust, and hatred.

Individuals and nations that are disconnected from universal consciousness may view themselves as superior or more deserving than others. This leads to exploitation,

---

"An eye for an eye only ends up making the whole world blind."
- Mahatma Gandhi

oppression, and ultimately, conflict. The deeper connection to the universe and one another is forgotten, and what remains is a narrow, self-centered view of the world.

When the identification and sense of belonging to the whole is absent, the self-centered view dominates. The 'us versus them' mentality takes root, and it becomes much easier to justify conflict and war. It allows leaders and special interest groups with hidden agendas to manipulate us into thinking that we need to fight for resources and self-protection.

What is the right thing to do if the evil of war is necessary to deter a more destructive evil? While absolute non-violence is the rule, response to specific situations like World War - II initiated by Hitler can be morally complex.

Governments need to protect their people from ruthless subjugation of evil aggressors. International bodies like the United Nations seek to preserve a relative state of peace. If a nation uses force to fulfill its lust for power, domination, exploitation of resources or simply to impose an ideological agenda by violating the rule of peaceful coexistence, even the UN charter may allow physical force by nations to defend themselves. The consequences otherwise may be more disastrous.

We need to reflect and find a middle path while ensuring that our main motive is not self-interest. Even at a personal level there may be compromises while fulfilling duties in daily life. The test of integrity here is the refusal

---

"We can never obtain peace in the outer world until we make peace with ourselves" - His Holiness the Dalai Lama

to subordinate moral conduct to narrow self-interest. For example, if a policeman, in pursuit of his duty, has to act aggressively to save the lives of innocent people, we normally don't consider that as an unwholesome action.

If we need to stop the brute aggression of a tyrant, unfortunately, we may have to participate in a defensive war to avoid the loss of more innocent lives. We may have to navigate the moral predicament, examine our own motives and take an appropriate stand to minimize harm and suffering for those at risk. In this context transformation at an individual level becomes more significant.

In the *Bhagavad Gita*, one of the most revered Hindu scriptures, Lord Krishna suggests that Arjuna should engage in war only after he nurtures calmness and peace within and be free from anger, hate, vengeance, and urge to express his strength or superiority. He calls for courage and resolve to fight a just war by following his duty, even if it leads to painful consequences.

He however recommends an attitude to ensure that conduct is not driven by emotions such as anger, ill will, and hatred. Krishna further emphasizes the need for peace, love, compassion, a deep sense of oneness with all of creation and a transcendental vision to face the challenges of life with clarity and confidence.

However, the teachings of Buddha are clear that we should stay away from wars in all conditions. He suggested

---

"Peace cannot be kept by force; it can only be achieved by understanding." - Albert Einstein that we can have peace only through a collective consciousness of love and goodwill.

Path to Peace, Way Forward:

We need to build a world where war is no longer an option and where peace and prosperity are possible for all. The boundaries we create around social symbols such as nation, religion, and race are constructs of human minds and products of history and culture. But these divisions are not real in the natural world as they don't exist in the physical realm.

We must move beyond the false divisions of race, nationality, and religion and understand that we are all part of the same human family sharing this planet and its resources. We must work toward developing empathy and understanding for others, especially those who are suffering. Compassion is the antidote to craving and aversion.

Awareness of the consequences of our actions, both on the individual and collective level, is crucial in creating a more just and peaceful world. We must consciously choose to address our differences with dialogue, negotiation, and cooperation rather than with hatred, fear, or violence.

We are all part of the same human family with shared aspirations, struggles, and dreams. We are connected not only to each other but to all other forms of life on Earth and beyond. A borderless world offers a profound way of

---

"Imagine all the people living life in peace. You may say that I'm a dreamer, but I'm not the only one. I hope someday you'll join us and the world will be as one." - John Lennon

"World peace must develop from inner peace. Peace is not just mere absence of violence. Peace is, I think, the manifestation of human compassion." - His Holiness the Dalai Lama

thinking about our place in the world and our relationship with all forms of existence. So, the path to peace starts with peace at an individual level.

Peace is not something we attain - it is something we cultivate. When we embody love, compassion, and equanimity, peace is no longer a distant goal but a living reality. When our intentions and thoughts are pure, everything else will fall in place; success will follow; peace reigns with love, joy, caring, and celebration for all beings who learn to live in harmony.

Buddha's noble eightfold path is simple and more practical for transformation at an individual level. This in turn is likely to transform collective consciousness among a significant number of people all over the world with a positive impact for peace on Mother Earth.

"Do your little bit of good where you are; it's those little bits of good put together that overwhelm the world." - Desmond Tutu

Chapter Three

Path of Purification

"Our life is shaped by our mind; we become what we think. Suffering follows an evil thought as the wheels of a cart follow the oxen that draws it."

- Buddha

The path of purification is an organized, systematic presentation of the teachings of Buddha in a clear and comprehensive manner. The noble eightfold path is the path of purification leading to enlightenment and liberation from suffering by cultivating morality, mindfulness, and insight through practices like right understanding, right intention, and right concentration.

Buddha described the path in simple terms while explaining the path to an elderly woman as below:

Abstain from all sinful, unwholesome actions,
Perform only pious wholesome ones,
Purify the mind.
That is the teaching of enlightened ones.

Prince Siddhartha Gautama was born into the Sankhya clan in the foothills of the Himalayas, sometime between 563 and 483 BC. Seeing the unhappiness, sickness, and death in human life, he became a sincere seeker of the ultimate truth and a way out of human suffering. He abandoned the royal life in search of a higher truth at an young age of 29. Buddha as Siddhartha later became known, developed teachings and practices based on the profound insight of enlightenment experienced at the age of 35.

With a noble mission to share his experiences and wisdom with the common people, he spent the rest of his life

---

"Nothing is more precious than peace. Nothing brings more happiness. Peace is the most basic starting point for the advancement of humankind." - Buddha

"All compounded things are subject to decay. Strive hard with diligence and heedfulness for your own salvation." - Buddha

through the formulation and clear exposition of what came to be known as the 'path or way'. For 45 long years, till his ripened end, the portals of his teachings were open for any seeker, irrespective of caste, creed, race, and earlier affiliations.

The first teaching by Buddha after his enlightenment was through the maiden discourse named 'Turning of the Wheel'. It advocated a middle path that steers clear of extremes of life of indulgence and one of harsh austerity. His teachings serve as a major guide that will enable people towards freedom, emancipation, and wholeness with freshness like the 'life of flowers'.

The hallmark of his approach was that enlightenment is one's personal experience. Buddha said, 'Be a lamp unto yourself', which means that each individual must walk one's own path to enlightenment. Along with the 'responsibility', this enabled the seeker, a 'freedom' of treading the 'way' as one evolves. Thus, a teacher can only be a guide or a mentor, showing the way, not doing the real work for them. An intellectual understanding of his teachings is helpful for inspiration. But walking the path with sustained practice, being a 'lamp unto oneself' can only develop purity of mind and noble qualities in a seeker.

The moderation in life, tolerance for personal choices in the spiritual path and the open membership to any seeker were radical ideas unlike regimentation. The community of seekers had the freedom of one's own sprouting and

---

"When the mind is pure, joy follows like a shadow that never leaves." - Buddha

blossomed like flowers. Mutual respect and tolerance were considered inherent. Thus, his teachings like a garden of flowers retained relevance dynamically with innate freshness like those of flowers in the nature.

Three marks of existence:

According to Buddha understanding the three universal truths referred to as 'Three marks of existence' is essential. Buddha taught that all phenomena of existence (objects, thoughts, and feelings) are marked by three characteristics - suffering, impermanence, and non-self. Nothing remains constant even for the smallest measurable moment as everything is in a state of flux.

Suffering (*Dukha*):

Buddha stated that suffering exists; there is a cause for suffering; the cause is craving, and the way to end suffering is the noble eightfold path. The concept and postulate of 'cause and effect' are fundamental to the teachings of Buddha.

On the issues of 'suffering', the 'Four Noble Truths' enunciated are:

i. Truth of suffering: There is suffering in the cycle of life and death.
ii. The truth of the cause of suffering: Craving is the cause of suffering.

"Peace is to be found in the same place as agitation and suffering. Where you experience suffering you can also find freedom from suffering." - Venerable Ajahn Chah

iii. The truth of the end of suffering: Suffering can end by cessation of craving.
iv. The truth of the path to end suffering: The path to end the suffering is by practicing the ways of the noble eight fold path.

The four truths do not deny happiness or simple joys in life but indicate that they too are transient and passing like all phenomena.

The word 'noble' as an adjective here has significance. It indicates that true 'nobility' is caused by the practitioner through moral actions, rather than by accident of birth.

Suffering can be due to the compulsive and intense craving for physical satisfaction of one sort or another. Suffering can also arise due to notional attributes such as attachment to things like a sense of self, individuality, ideas, opinions, beliefs, and values which are impermanent as nothing is enduring.

Interestingly, suffering arises as a consequence of attachment to belief in the existence of an enduring "I" and the concept of permanence. Suffering also happens when one does not get what one wants and when nothing seems enough; when one is separated from things that one likes or conjoined with things one dislikes.

The solution for freedom from cravings, aversions and bondage to identity of self is to develop experiential understanding of impermanence on a sustained basis;

"No one saves us but ourselves. No one can and no one may. We ourselves must walk the path." - Buddha particularly that of the five aggregates - body, consciousness, perception, feelings, and habitual mental dispositions.

Impermanence (*Anitya*):

All compounded things including physical and mental phenomena are impermanent. If one perceives and feels this truth by insight, he can be free from suffering. This is the path of purification. Impermanence is the rising, passing, and changing of everything, any phenomena related to mind and matter. Everything keeps changing every moment - arising, disappearing, and dissolving.

The 'Life of a Flower' illuminates as an analogy here. Flowers start with the germination of a seed, followed by the growth of a plant and the formation of buds which then bloom as flowers. The process of pollination ensures seeds for the continuation of life. With death and decay, flowers go back to earth as nutrients in a different form, for a new cycle. The repeating cycle is dynamic and no single stage is permanent.

The cognitive perception to experience this truth is *Anitya Sanna* (*Sanna* is a Pali word for cognitive perception). If the insight of *Anitya* becomes spontaneous and internalized, everything is perceived as a wave and all the five aggregates - body, consciousness, perception, feeling, and mental dispositions - are also transitory.

In *Vipassana*, one is trained to observe objectively with equanimity and detachment the sensations in the body

---

"Impermanent indeed are all conditioned things; they are of the nature of arising and passing away. Having come into being, they cease to exist." - Buddha

(*Vedana*), the state of mind (*Chitta*), the contents of the mind (*Dhamma*) and the body itself with a sustained experiential understanding of impermanence. It is not the consciousness, perception, feeling, and mental dispositions which are transitory that make one suffer. It is wanting things to be permanent when they are not that makes one suffer.

Non-self (*Anatta*):

Mere suffering exists, no sufferer is found.
The deeds are, but no doer of the deeds is there.
Nirvana is, but not the person that enters it;
The path is, but no traveler on it is seen.
[from the *Visuddhimagga* (path to purity)] -- by *Buddhaghosa*

The teaching of non-self is unique to the teachings of Buddha in the sense that there is no abiding fixed entity, no permanent, unchanging, or inherent 'self' or soul within individuals or phenomena, but rather a constantly changing stream of interconnected experiences.

Every moment there exists cognition followed by perception. The body and mind are more like processes as almost everything in our body and in the mind changes continuously, at every moment. The body is not the self, feelings are not the self, perceptions and the activities of consciousness are not the self.

"I... an universe of atoms, an atom in the universe." - Richard P. Feynman

"Morality, concentration and wisdom - the path of purification for cessation of suffering." - Buddha

Buddha taught that what we perceive as 'self' is actually a collection of five impermanent aggregates: form, perception, feeling, mental formations, and consciousness. But the mind includes anything and everything in the "I" to make it the most significant within all experiences and feelings. In a way, "I" becomes a block in the free flow of life through us.

It is important to clarify that 'non-self' does not mean denying the existence of individuals or phenomena, but rather the absence of a fixed, permanent self within them.

Noble eightfold path:

Buddha's noble eightfold path is a beacon of hope paving the path to become free from suffering. From the day of the maiden sermon, the wheel of *Dhamma* was set to motion for one of the greatest schools of thought in human history. This was widely accepted by scholars, emperors, and common people with overwhelming love and compassion. The interlinked eight spokes represent the core framework of the noble eightfold path.

All actions are motivated by volition for positive contribution and touching other's lives with clarity of thought. This path is a way of life with eight practices to follow and they are: right understanding, right intention, right speech, right action, right livelihood, right effort, right mindfulness, and right concentration.

"Just as the great ocean has one taste, the taste of salt, so also this teaching and discipline has one taste, the taste of liberation."
- Buddha

Short description of the eight factors:

Right Speech:

Abstaining from lying, abstaining from slander and backbiting, abstaining from harsh words and from frivolous talk is called right speech. It is also speaking the truth politely, appropriate to the context only when it is considered beneficial.

Right speech today could mean pausing before responding to a challenging email or disagreement, ensuring your words build harmony instead of division.

Right Action:

Abstaining from killing, abstaining from taking what is not given and abstaining from sexual misconduct is called right action.

Right Livelihood:

Avoiding professions that are unwholesome and earning livelihood by wholesome actions is the right livelihood.

Right Effort:

To inhibit and restrain immoral thoughts; to volitionally cause good thoughts and to nurture already prevailing positive, wholesome thoughts is the right effort.

"If you know how to let go and be at peace, you know everything you need to know about living in the world."
- Venerable Ajahn Brahm

Right Mindfulness:

To observe objectively body in body, mind in mind, mental objects in mental objects, and sensation in sensations with equanimity and a thorough understanding of impermanence is the right mindfulness.

Right Concentration:

Practicing different stages of sustained attention leading to absorption culminating in tranquility, insight, and equanimity, to dwell in equanimity with sustained application of mind and awareness of impermanence is the right concentration.

Right View:

The knowledge about cause and effect, the suffering, the arising of suffering, the ceasing of suffering, and the way leading to the cessation of suffering is the right view. It is the way of seeing things as they are, rather than what they appear to be. It is insight grasped at the deeper level of the mind with the understanding of impermanence and non-self.

Right Thoughts:

Thoughts of renunciation, love, kindness, and thoughts free from aversion and violence are right thoughts.

Each part of the noble eightfold path falls within three groups: which are *Sila* (Morality) comprising right speech,

---

"Impermanent are all compounded things. When one perceives this with insight, then one becomes detached from suffering - this is the path of purification." - Buddha

"Every breath we take, every step we make, can be filled with peace, joy and serenity" - Thich Nhat Hanh

right action, and right livelihood; *Samadhi* (Meditation) comprising right effort, right mindfulness, and right concentration; *Panna* (Wisdom) comprising right view and right thought. The eightfold path is integrated and comprehensive like eight folds on a single cloth.

Garden of Wisdom:

Gardens bloom in bright colors.
Flowers sway in the morning light.
Pure and bright, bathed in love and light.
Celebration of life with sympathetic joy.

Long ago, a wise old sage lived in a flower garden. It had a pond and many trees; adjoining was a river flowing towards a forest. The sage who was inspired by Buddha in his life, often shared his wisdom, gained over the years.

Young Aswajith felt disturbed in his life. He was worldly successful in achieving fame, power, and wealth. But a war in his country which ravaged thousands had deeply hurt him.

He was sad with empathy for the suffering of those affected by the war caused by greed for power, wealth, and domination. He came to meet the revered monk, to seek his blessings and listen to words of wisdom with the hope of finding the right path to peace and happiness. He sought

---

"The happiness of your life depends upon the quality of your thoughts." - Marcus Aurelius

peace and wanted to regain equanimity; wanted to learn the ways to be normal amidst the chaos. He desperately needed guidance from the revered monk and hence went to the garden to visit him.

One of the students guided him through the garden of flowers. In the tranquil environs of the garden, after some refreshing food and rest, he was greeted by the smiling sage in the early evening along with others. It was a bright evening, with the wind whispering through the trees. The petals of flowers in the garden were soft, with varied colors. The mixture of fragrances was stimulating. In the tranquil moments, his mind became receptive, and he was ready for earnest listening.

Aswajith's first basic query was, "Teacher, I feel all I need is peace. Is it possible for a householder to follow Buddha's path?"

The teacher's eyes showed empathy. Kindness was in his face. He nodded and took out a small seed from his pouch and held it up for all to see and said, "This seed is the seed of life. The seed holds the potential to become a flower, a fruit, or a tree. Similarly, each one of you, deep within yourself has the potential for peace. All of you for sure can develop compassion and love. But the seed needs to be nurtured. It must be planted in the soil of understanding, watered with love, and cared for with goodwill."

He continued, "Seek the truth from the nature. Observe in silence the graceful opening of the petals unfolding under

---

"You yourself must strive. The Buddhas only point the way."
- Buddha

the infinite sky. Feel it. In the grand design of existence, we are flowers of the universe, growing, changing, and trying to reach towards the infinity."

Gazing at the sky, Ashwajith felt the enormity of the overwhelming canopy. It was soothing and a secure feeling ensued. Some thoughts were evoked in him. The flowers in the garden seemed as if they had assimilated the teachings of Buddha. Each one appeared like a lesson. The monk smiled and gently persuaded, "Listen to the flowers and their whispers. They will guide you, silently but surely."

The monk wanted to elaborate on the specifics of paths, after generic metaphors. The seekers were awaiting the moment. They needed more details, precisely the reason why they visited.

"The noble eightfold path as taught by Buddha is a path that leads to the cessation of suffering. This path is a way of life, which needs eight practices to follow. But all are meaningful only in tandem and together. They are the right understanding, right intention, right speech, right action, right livelihood, right effort, right mindfulness, and right concentration."

Looking at the cluster of different flowers, he stressed, "Each element of the path in the spiritual journey is vital by itself. They are all like folds in the same cloth or petals of the same flower." He pointed to a beautiful lotus flower as if to answer Ashwajith's earlier doubt. He said, "The lotus represents the purity of the heart. Just as the lotus grows

---

"Dwell on the beauty of life. Watch the stars, and see yourself running with them." - Marcus Aurelius

"Without suffering, you have no ways in order to learn how to be understanding and compassionate." - Thich Nhat Hanh

through the entangling mud, one can have peace amidst household life. The ego and attachments are impediments. Peace can be attained through mindfulness and the right actions through practice of the eightfold path.

Aswajith watched the lotus as it swayed gently in the breeze and realized that his own life had often been clouded by struggles and desires, much like the mud in which the lotus was rooted. But the lotus showed him that, despite his past, he too, could rise with purity, if only he could let go of his attachments.

The teacher appeared to be sober and was hinting at a detailed session. All the seekers were attentive as they did not want to miss anything. The monk began with the seed, pointing to a tiny bud at the base of the flower. "Right understanding is like the seed of the flower. It is the insight to slowly assimilate reality, the reality of impermanence. Also, by being mindful, one starts realizing that sufferings are due to strong attachments. Every learning is incremental. Right understanding, nevertheless is the beginning of the spiritual journey and it seeps gradually like diffusion. This is true for any step in the eightfold path", he cautioned.

After a pause, he moved on to the next point. "Observe the sun shining on the flowers. The 'right intention' is like the sun, providing motive and direction of growth to flowers. Without sunlight there will not be any growth. Right intentions are motivations. They are yearning for compassion

---

"Very little is needed to make a happy life; it is all within yourself in your way of thinking." - Marcus Aurelius

and wishing to be free from ill will. Intentions are powerful drives for sustenance. As a by-product, over a long period, one learns the value of collective growth of all."

"Right speech is an art, for positive interactions", the monk said without hesitation. "Cultivate speaking truthfully, for harmony, using a gentle and kind tone. Speak mindfully to ensure that words are useful and purposeful. This is going to be helpful in spiritual growth and purification of mind." He also indicated to abstain consciously from false, divisive, and abusive speech.

Aswajith understood that right speech is like the gentle breeze that moves through the garden carrying with it the fragrance of flowers, which uplifts the spirit. He further realized that speech with words based on truth, which is beneficial, kind, and polite will nurture harmony.

The 'right action' is the fourth element of the noble eightfold path, emphasizing ethical conduct and avoiding actions that cause harm, such as killing and stealing. To make his point, the monk turned to a beautiful iris flower, its petals just beginning to open up and said, "The gentle unfolding of the petals suggests the way we should live and act. Our choices and actions should be like the opening of petals." He further highlighted, "Your actions should be contributing to a peaceful and harmonious environment, both internally and externally. It should be ethical and promote beneficial action to all."

Aswajith was wondering how we humans are harming

"There are only two mistakes one can make along the road to truth; not going all the way, and not starting." - Buddha ourselves and causing misery to millions due to actions that lead to wars. Minds enslaved by greed for power, arrogance, and conceit are causing immense suffering.

"Right livelihood is quite simple on the face of it; one's occupation shall not cause harm to others. Avoid those that involve activities like weapons dealing, slavery, or exploiting others", the monk declared.

Aswajith started reflecting on his profession where he was highly successful, made millions and earned respect. Unfortunately, his work also caused harm to many innocent people as he worked in defense research to develop arms. He felt that his work should not harm others directly or indirectly and instead it should lead to the well-being of all. He understood that true happiness comes from honest, meaningful work that benefits others.

He wondered which was more important: playing an active role in defending national integrity even if it causes suffering or staying away from it? He realized that the right thing to do is to bring light that dispels darkness through positive actions which promotes peace and well-being.

The monk continued, "Right effort is a simple concept. It is to consciously cultivate positive mental states and avoid negative ones. Right effort is crucial for spiritual progress and achieving enlightenment because it actively shapes the mind and cultivates a positive path toward well-being and liberation. It needs diligence and persistent intent."

"Nurture your soul by engaging in virtuous acts; watch your inner garden flourish." - Buddha

"Do not dwell in the past, do not dream of the future, concentrate the mind on the present moment" - Buddha

The monk walked towards the pond and gestured towards the reflection of the sky in the clear, still water. He said, "Just as the pond reflects the sky perfectly when still, our minds must remain clear to reflect reality as it is. Mindfulness brings clarity, bringing us into direct contact with the present moment." Further, he said that it should lead to 'Right concentration' which is a state of sustained awareness of reality such as one's own natural breath.

Aswajith requested the monk to throw more light on right mindfulness for his better understanding.

The monk explained, "Right mindfulness is the ability to be present in every moment, to observe our thoughts, actions, and feelings without attachment or judgment. We must learn to be fully present, accepting life as it comes. To be 'Present' or 'Just Being' is so important to celebrate life with real happiness."

Finally, the monk pointed to the whole garden, where all the flowers stood together in harmony. He said harmony happens with purity of intentions and actions. For that we need to gain mastery over our minds and purify them with the right mindfulness and right concentration. Through meditation, we unite all aspects of the path into a harmonious whole.

Aswajith sat quietly, the entire garden unfolding before him as if whole nature was in a meditative state. He realized that the right concentration was the way to integrate all the teachings into a single, unified experience of being.

"If you have to choose between being kind and being right, choose being kind and you will always be right." - Buddha

As the sun set behind the mountains, Aswajith felt a deep sense of connection to the flowers, Buddha's path and the world around him. He felt a quiet calm settle in his heart. His heart was full of gratitude and wisdom with the understanding that the way of flowers is one of deep connection, balance, and peace.

He understood now that the noble eightfold path wasn't just a set of teachings; it was a living, breathing cycle, much like the flowers themselves - each part essential, each one a reflection of the whole. Each flower in the garden is a living reminder of Buddha's wisdom, showing Aswajith that by aligning with the natural rhythms of life, he can find peace and enlightenment. It became clear to him that the spiritual path is a voyage that requires cautious treading and conscious attempts. However, it needs guidance and support from the right teachers who act like glowing lamps.

The monk concluded his sermon with the final words, "Walking this path should result in the development of qualities of loving-kindness, compassion, altruistic joy and equanimity with the removal of ego, hatred and ill will at the deepest level of mind." The matured sermon along with the heavenly surroundings of flowers in the garden had a salutary effect.

Aswajith felt peaceful but understood that it was a long voyage to reach a sustained state of equanimity and peace. He felt confident that Buddha's eightfold path could make his life peaceful and meaningful.

"First remove I, that's Ego; then remove want, that's Desire. See now you are left with only Happiness." - Buddha

Chapter Four

We Are All One

"An 'open heart' is spacious presence, in which the sense of separateness between yourself and the 'other' dissolves and there is the recognition of oneness, of shared consciousness. That recognition is love."

- Eckhart Tolle

"All things arise because of their interdependence, and that is why nothing has a separate, independent identity." - Thich Nhat Hanh

Introduction:

The profound teachings of saints and spiritual thinkers remain relevant. They offer balance and moderation amidst the stress and restlessness of the modern way of life. The pursuit of ever-increasing aspirations and pleasures of life is causing fear and anxiety. Many of us started looking for ways and means to develop inner peace.

Spirituality is a rational and critical inquiry into the nature of 'self' and its place in the universe through observation and experimentation 'within', while science is based on observation and experimentation 'without'. Religion is in a way a tool to become spiritual and ultimately help people to become a better version of themselves.

Science also explores nature to harness and control the resources for mankind. It is the intellectual and the 'analytical description' of different aspects of nature. It may be a worthwhile effort to view the cursory details of present day scientific knowledge and also ancient wisdom shared by sages based on their personal experiences.

Amazing are the similarities during the analysis, among the science and the insights shared by many enlightened ones. It may be noted here that teachings themselves are like a flowing river, meant to assimilate the new strides dynamically while simultaneously being enriched.

"In the sky there is no distinction of east and west; people create distinctions out of their own minds and then believe them to be true." - Buddha

Scientific perspective:

The Cosmic realm covers the large scale structures of the universe like the planets, the stars, and the galaxies formed by the aggregation of matter over the vast distances and timescales. The behavior of structures including the gravitational forces and the energy that hold them together is by a smooth fabric of space and time. This is described by Einstein's theory of general relativity.

M-theory tries to offer a unified model. This model provides the possibility of integrating a four-dimensional model of existence suitable for intelligent life such as humans based on anthropic principle and multi-dimensional reality at the quantum level. It proposes that we live in a 'brane' with a four-dimensional surface along with curled up six or seven dimensions of space time like a filled sphere or nutshell. The gravity that spreads into the extra dimension together with other branes may interact to produce multiple universes and we happen on a brane suitable for intelligent life to evolve.

The ekpyrotic universe model suggests that the universe we are aware of is the current version of an infinite cycle of universes stretching into the past and the future. It suggests the 'Big Bang' as a moment at which the universe slowly contracted to an incredibly small point and bounced to expansion. From the moment of the Big Bang, it took about seven days to create the universe we are in today. The journey started with the formation of bosons, followed by

---

"Quantum physics thus reveals a basic oneness of the universe."
- Erwin Schrodinger

quarks, hydrons (protons, neutrons), and leptons (electrons, photons). Then, nucleosynthesis happened with formation of atomic nuclei leading to nuclei of deuterium and helium. All this happened in the first three minutes. The expansion of the universe further leads to the formation of galaxies, stars, and planets.

Everything in the universe appears to be a multi-dimensional ever changing dynamic flow of interconnected fields of fundamental forces, rather than a static combination of individual entities. The universe is associated with expansion and contraction at different times with a good possibility of multiple universes and the absence of singularity. This understanding should help us to look at this universe as an interconnected whole that transcends space and time.

Classic to Quantum:

Science, particularly Physics can be viewed from the perspective of reality at micro as well as macro levels. The 'micro' deals with those aspects of the universe such as fundamental particles and the 'macro' enfolds the vastness of the planets, the galaxies, and the universe.

At the beginning of the twentieth century classical physics was good enough to explain phenomena from interstellar distances planets, stars, and galaxies covering stars down to the hundredth of a millimeter covering basic

---

"The atoms or elementary particles themselves are not real; they form a world of potentialities or possibilities rather than one of things or facts." - Werner Heisenberg

NASA's James Webb Space Telescope image of stars and galaxies as they appeared 13 billion years ago

"No self is of itself alone. It has a long chain of intellectual ancestors. The "I" is chained to ancestry by many factors…This is not mere allegory, but an eternal memory." - Erwin Schrodinger

building blocks of matter called atoms. An adult human is made up of around seven octillion atoms and most of the space in each atom is empty though solidity is experienced because of inter-atomic bonding.

Later research in atomic physics led to the discovery of electrons, protons, neutrons, and even smaller particles called quarks and our understanding of their behavior at lengths down to the billionths of a millimeter. The smallest building blocks of matter like the quarks, the leptons, and the bosons are the foundation of the universe at the micro level.

The behavior of the matter, including the forces and the energy at this scale, is governed by the principles of quantum mechanics which describes phenomena like the wave-particle duality and the quantization. The quantum field theory proposes that all particles and the forces arising from the quantum fields, permeate the entire universe implying a common underlying fabric of reality.

The subatomic particles can connect across vast distances transcending limits of space and time. The subatomic particles can be entangled, meaning they can be instantaneously connected across vast distances defying the limits of space and time, deeply interconnected, no matter how distant they appear. Quantum tunneling explains the process of the relation and interactions between the micro and the macro domains - like the light enabling photosynthesis.

"Consciousness cannot be accounted for in physical terms. For consciousness is absolutely fundamental. It cannot be accounted for in terms of anything else." - Erwin Schrodinger

So, at the fundamental level, all things are connected in a continual dance of energy, vibration, and potentiality. This calls for a paradigm shift in the understanding of reality from parts to whole, objects to relationships, and content to patterns. Further, the relationships are non-linear consisting of multiple feedback loops. Change in one relationship may lead to change in the ever-widening patterns amplified by independent feedback loops.

This constant flux mirrors the idea of impermanence in spiritual philosophies where nothing is truly separate or permanent and everything is in a state of becoming. The universe is a vast interconnected field of energy, where everything is linked and there is no truly independent existence - just as in spiritual thought all things are ultimately expressions of a single, undivided reality.

Human Ecology:

The universe operates on the fundamental principles of interconnectedness, where all forms of matter and energy are continuously transforming, flowing, and interacting. The web of life is based on a vast and intricate network of vrelationships among all members of the ecological community including plants, animals, and micro-organisms.

In nature every life form, from the tiniest micro-organisms to the largest animals, plays a role in the broader network of life. The plants absorb sunlight, animals eat the

---

"The final goal of all religions is to realise the essential oneness."
- Mahatma Gandhi

plants, decomposers break down organic material, and the nutrients cycle back into the soil. Humans are part of this web, just as much as every other form of life. Earth, as a living system functions like a single, holistic, interconnected, self-regulating organism that does not fit neatly into the boundaries humans have drawn for themselves.

Humanity is part of a larger ecosystem of life and every individual - regardless of where they come from. Every being is formed from the same basic building blocks of life and our very existence depends on the same natural processes that sustain every other life form on Earth.

When walking through a forest, can we sense our deep bond with the trees, rivers, and wildlife, reminding ourselves that we too are threads in this intricate web?

We are all a family as we share the genes of our ancestors and all of us are related in some way or other. Genes are part of our DNA which defines the way each and every part of our body grows and functions including neurons in our brain. Further 99.9 percent of genes in every cell are the same for all human beings and we share most of them with other animals too.

The mutual dependence of all life processes on one another is obvious. The survival and success of each member of the ecological community depends on the success of the whole community and vice versa.

"If kindness is imagined as a beautiful dove, then wisdom is its wings. Compassion without wisdom never takes off."
- Venerable Ajahn Brahm

"Be at peace in the oneness of things, and all errors will disappear by themselves." - Jianzhi Sengcan

Ancient Wisdom:

Like modern physics, ancient wisdom points to the interconnectedness of all things. The concept of non-duality informed by many sages in spiritual tradition is the idea that all distinctions we make (between self and other, subject and object, mind and body) are ultimately illusions. At the deepest level of reality, everything is one. They all tried to explain the path to transcendent experience of the state of enlightenment, a reality transcending all realms of phenomenal existence with the cessation of the mental formations. No one could find the words to adequately describe the state of enlightenment or *Nirvana* as it is not causally conditioned and is beyond existence as well as non-existence. This may perhaps be explained in terms of pure awareness that is free from the influence of all aggregates of mind and matter including cognition, perception, feelings, and mental formations.

According to mystics from all over the world, enlightenment reveals that everything including all forms of mind and matter are manifestations of the same ultimate reality which some refer to as pure awareness. However, they could not explain it in words as it is a state of being that is indescribable just like happiness and the description of happiness being different.

The concept of non-duality proposed by revered sages in India is that all distinctions, including the dichotomy observed in the real world are ultimately illusions. At

---

"The essence of spirituality is, to be constantly aware of the oneness of all; at the same time to celebrate the uniqueness of the individual." - Jaggi Vasudev

the deepest level of reality, everything is one unified consciousness. The ultimate truth is an unaffected, undifferentiated purity that is ineffable and hence can only be experienced. This school of thought posits that pure consciousness is the ultimate reality. It is the diffused, conditioned, scattered consciousness that permeates the world. The experience of ultimate truth is considered inexplicable, and difficult to define but sages tried to explain it through pointers.

All this is full. All that is full.
From fullness, fullness comes.
When fullness is taken from fullness,
fullness still remains.
......Isha Upanishad

The *Isha Upanishad* further explains that it is neither knowing nor unknowing, nor even knowingness; it is ineffable, beyond thought, indefinable - neither seen nor understood, neither inner nor outer awareness, not even the suspension of awareness. It is neither existence nor nonexistence, and it is known only through becoming it.

Some scholars described this as a state of absolute emptiness; there is no time, no space, no becoming, no thingness. It is an experience of pure mind seeing itself as reflected.

"In the momentous instants of ending of 'solitude muse', his identity as 'Self' dissolved with the enormity, transcending his awareness. It was 'Everything' and 'Nothing'." - Ambale Naga

It is also referred to as pure awareness or pure consciousness through which everything is known. Human consciousness involves perception, reason, feeling, remembering, and imagining as well as the ability to access and use information for reasoning and decision making.

Pure consciousness here refers to a state of being free from modes of mind, free from valid, invalid, and distorted perceptions of reality, mental notions, impressions, tendencies, sleep, and memories. This represents a state where the knower, known, and the process of knowing becomes one with the absence of any witness. This is also referred to as pure awareness, the ever-present unchanging reality transcending the distinction between existence and nonexistence.

Through the 'mind' only, such a truth can be reached and hence it must be guarded and purified. Knowing about the mind, its purification, and the control becomes the paramount and dominant activity in the seeker's path. The morals and ethics along with discipline are the initial prerequisites. The light of compassion and unconditioned love present in every being is radiated once the clouds of impurities like ego, hatred, and ill will which arise out of delusion are removed.

The real exploration starts with the meditation practices of mindfulness to feel the processes of the body and mind. The practice is in sync with the observation of natural breath. Thus, the creativity of the mind working on itself becomes favorable as the mind gets progressively subtler and

---

"The way is not in the sky. The way is in the heart." - Buddha

"Love is the recognition of oneness in the world of duality."
- Eckhart Tolle

purer. Meditation with the right mindfulness is a process of purification from moment to moment.

In the teachings of Buddha, this experience of ultimate truth is referred to as *Nirvana*. It is the cessation of the suffering with the ceasing of the cravings, the aversions, and the delusions. It is considered an ineffable experience beyond mind, matter, and phenomena. It is a state wherein the observer, observed and even the observation process dissolves as it is known only through 'being'. It is pure consciousness...

The conspicuous resonance of thoughts and ideas among science, teaching of enlightened ones from different spiritual traditions and Buddha's perceptions is not by coincidence. The premise of Buddha's doctrines is enquiry and reasoning. His philosophy over centuries has evolved through observation, contemplation, and experiences. Notably, his teachings did not encourage dogmas or blind belief; instead it is nurtured by a free will for positive progress. Such an attitude was fertile for the iterative and incremental growth of its mature evolution.

Let us try to reflect on oneness through a story.

The Garden of Oneness:

In a peaceful village nestled between tall green mountains, a wise middle-aged woman following Buddha's teachings is living. Her name is Samatha. The garden is a peaceful place and has a plethora of flowers, in a mix of

---

"What we observe is not nature itself, but nature exposed to our method of questioning." - Werner Heisenberg

variety but blooming together. Their dance to the tunes of breeze is a sight to watch. One day during the spring, three teenagers Muditha, Maithri, and Karuna visited the garden.

The girls, soon after entering the garden, were in disbelief. The aroma of white jasmines turned their heads; the bright red gulmohar, gerbera daisy spruced in red, yellow and pink shades were elegant.

The rose flowers in hues were a dream to watch; the majestic yellow-gold sunflowers and rustic marigolds in orange and yellow were captivating. It was an ineffable experience. The sight of an exquisite pink and white lotus in the pond, the symbol of enlightenment and prosperity, was divine stunning. They are lost in the magical spell, absorbed in the beauty, serenity, and grandeur of the garden of flowers.

For Muditha, all the flowers blooming together was unbelievable. In all curiosity she asked the gardener, "How do the flowers bloom together in sync?"

Samatha with a smile said, "It is Nature's orderliness and ordain; there maybe many hidden messages to humans, perhaps. In nature, the different flowers unique in traits appear to be complementing each other. They bloom at once.; They retain uniqueness in color, shape, and fragrance and yet they share togetherness. They simply bloom as they are, sharing their beauty with the world as each flower adds something special to the whole. Don't

---

"To plant a garden is to believe in tomorrow." - Audrey Hepburn

you think it is tacit and implied advice from nature to humans?"

For all it sounded logical.

Meanwhile, Muditha wondered, "Why don't we get inspired from flowers? Even though we are different in many ways, if we can learn to live together, the world can be a garden of peace." Muditha's heart was filled with warmth as she sat in the garden surrounded by the beauty of nature. She felt that true peace is not a distant dream and it can be nurtured in the way we live, in the way we treat one another, in the way we embrace our uniqueness and come together as one.

Samatha continued, "The tragedy of the present world is, we have created isolated blocks in living. We no longer feel the nuances of nature. Our faculty to observe and learn is forgotten."

Karuna enquired, "How can we get inspired by nature to feel together?"

Samatha responded, "The way of flowers is a classic example, in front of you. Like flowers, there are so many manifestations we can see in nature. The clouds which bring rain may have traveled across mountains to water the plants and the sunlight the plants receive have come from stars, billions of miles away. They are all part of the same energy web. The plants, the soil, the sun, and the rain

---

"The noblest pleasure is the joy of understanding." - Leonardo da Vinci

"We are all one. When we allow ourselves to become aware of this statement in its purest form, we open the doors to reveal the oneness of being." - Jim Harrison

are all part of a great, invisible dance. Are not all entities in the world in a matrix of connectivity?"

Karuna felt a warm sense of oneness in her heart. She understood that the world is a place where everything, whether a seed in the ground or a star in the sky, is part of a grand, unified whole. The idea of a multi-dimensional matrix of togetherness and unity of a wide range of apparently diverse elements in the universe, living and nonliving things, visible and invisible was overwhelming.

Samatha, perhaps to show another glaring attribute of nature, slowly led them to the flowing stream. They sat on the banks observing the soothing flow of water. In the quietness, the young girls started listening to the soft murmur of the water. They watched the movements of water, sometimes slow and steady; other times rushing faster, even navigating around the rocks.

Maithri felt that the stream was conveying some messages. She enquired, "What wisdom the stream is trying to convey? One thing I can perceive surely is that, though the flow appears steady, I can feel there are variations in undercurrents."

Samatha smiled, "The water in the river is like the flow of consciousness - always flowing, but importantly, always changing. The river is a perfect symbol of the world we observe. The apparent manifested reality in the world appears to be unchanging but with all its infinite forms,

---

"The reality we can put into words is never reality itself." - Werner Heisenberg

it is in constant flux. Everything is changing and hence impermanent."

Samatha even added another dimension, which the girls never imagined. "As your exposure to nature gets sensitized, you perceive that everything arises from the same unmanifested source, the pure energy." All stood up along with the elderly lady, gazing at the river and cherishing their newfound revelations. They felt their life was in an eternal flow, along with that of nature. Now, they felt a stronger bond with nature.

Karuna did not stop. "If the flower isn't permanent, does that mean it has no real identity? Is it truly a 'flower'?"

Samatha did not expect this question. Her face softened. "Wow, you are touching on a very deep concept; the concept of 'non-self'. In my limitation, I will try to explain."

She pointed to the flower. "This flower may appear as a single, independent thing to our eyes, but it is made up of many parts - the petals, the stem, the roots. And interestingly, all of these are connected to the earth, the air, the sunlight, and the water. Thus, the identity of flowers arises from a vast network of interconnections as part of ever-changing flow of life.

Samatha smiled, "The flower's form, our forms, including all are temporary amalgams only, in the cycle. 'Self' is a notional identity. All forms are interconnected elements and indeed, temporary."

"Whatever your circumstances, whatever your past, the forces that determine your future are nowhere but within your own heart and mind. It is here that the star of your destiny shines." - Buddha

When Karuna looked at the garden, she could see blooming flowers, wilting ones, leaves shedding trees, and decayed fruits. Everything is changing and everything is impermanent. But that change is not the end. It's a transformation, a part of the ongoing dance of life. They arise, they exist for a time and then they return to the earth only to give rise to new life. This is the way of nature.

For the three young girls, it was an amazing experience full of revelations, new found realities, cherished peace, and happiness with the flowers and the garden. In gratitude, they all thanked Samatha. They felt peace with the understanding that they were not alone; they were part of something much greater.

"Because all existence is founded upon the ever-present state of union, everything already exists in a state of tranquility."
- Shunryu Suzuki

Chapter Five

Flower - The Way

"A flower's appeal is in its contradictions - so delicate in form yet strong in fragrance, so small in size yet big in beauty, so short in life yet long on effect."

- Buddha

Human civilization evolved based on the concept of an ideal society proposed by various philosophers of those times. The ideas from thinkers with varied schools of thought laid the foundation for evolution which endured changes and transformation.

The beauty, grace, and gentle nature of the flowers represent blissful emotions of purity, joy, and serenity. 'Flower the way' denotes the beautiful concept of brightening one's life, similar to that of a flower. The 'life of flowers' can become an inspiring model for humans to follow. It is Buddha's way.

A moment of thought, a fleeting glance, or even the tender fragrance of a flower in the mild breeze can have a salutary effect. That is the grandeur of flowers. A thing of beauty is a joy forever. Every flower is unique and beautiful in its own way. Despite their apparent differences, all the flowers innately belong to the same universal order. It is a subset of all the things in existence which are related and interconnected.

Flowers and the Cycle of Life:

Flowers embody the essence of the universe through their cycle of birth and senescence with a deep connection to the four fundamental elements - air, water, sunlight, and earth. A tiny seed, buried in the earth, awakens with the touch of water and absorbs nutrients. Slowly pushing through the soil, the roots anchor deep in the ground. Then starts its journey upwards to bloom with flowers.

"Happiness held is the seed. Happiness shared is the flower."
- John Harrigan

"As a bee gathering nectar does not harm or disturb the colour and fragrance of the flower; so do the wise move through the world."
- Buddha

A flower's way from the beginning to the end has stages of germination, roots and shoots, leaves, stems, and eventually flowers. As the bud unfurls, it drinks in sunlight changing it into energy, radiating beauty and fragrance. The air carries its scent inviting pollinators. The petals attract pollinators with their vibrant colors and scents as the allure of life. The sepals encase and protect the budding flower for foundational support. Stamens produce pollen, essential for fertilization. The pistil receives pollen and nurtures seed development.

The roots anchor the plant and absorb nutrients for grounding, stability, and the interconnecting of all life through the Earth's resources. The stem supports the flower and transports nutrients for the pathways of energy and sustenance that connect different aspects of life.

Flowers undergo senescence of aging to wilt and finally to death. Once a flower dies, decomposers like bacteria and fungi break down it's organic matter releasing nutrients back into the soil. It supports plant growth and maintains ecological balance.

This cyclical process exemplifies the interconnectedness of life and the continuous flow of energy and nutrients within the universe. This is valid for all entities including humans. Flowers embody the essence of the universe through their cycle of birth and senescence.

"Love is the flower you've got to let grow." - John Lennon

Flowers and the Culture:

As a natural evolution from ancient times, flowers are ingrained into our culture. They have been an inseparable entity within our beliefs, in the norms of rituals, in values, and in symbols. What they implicitly hint at during various occasions is more effective than the spoken words.

The floral symbols have been integral to art and literature as metaphors for human virtues and moral ideals. White Lilly is for purity and innocence, while Mint is for excellence and integrity. Violet exudes modesty and humility; Bluebell has a gentle disposition. White Rose is graceful with beauty; the Lotus, the king of flowers, is sacred at the altar of worship. The list is endless....

In literature the flowers are the poet's 'jewels', while for the artists, they are the 'ethereal dreams' swaying the human moods. Their enduring presence in cultural expressions underscores the deep connection between nature and human values.

Flowers for Inspiration:

Our blessed association with myriad flowers is as old as our conscious existence. In our childhood days in school, we recited poems by Wordsworth. In his bliss of solitude, he extols the pleasure the flowers fill in his heart. As children it was a memorable experience to enjoy the beauty of wildflowers on the roadside; those in the woods and fields.

"Love is like wildflowers; it's often found in the most unlikely places." - Ralph Waldo Emerson

Flowers, the bliss of nature, share their beauty and fragrance spontaneously with anyone without asking for anything in return. A flower doesn't ask for acknowledgment or reward; it simply exists to offer its gift. Giving is not just a virtue, but an experience that enriches both the giver and receiver. This selfless giving mirrors the compassionate act of offering help and unconditional love without any desire for personal gain - an act of love that heals with its quiet presence.

Flowers beautifully embody peace, serenity, and equanimity reflecting these qualities in their essence and presence. A blooming flower exists in quiet stillness at that moment. A lotus floating on tranquil waters or lavender swaying in a breeze exudes the serene energy that invites us to slow down, breathe and simply be. They are invaluable and inspiring virtue to 'embrace the moment' and 'just be'. Lotus rises from the muddy waters, untouched by its surroundings and the sunflower stands tall, turning towards the light. Their call to us is inspiring to be steady and graceful in life's rough times.

Flowers and the Nature:

The different entities, except humans, flourish in harmony under the age of nature. A flower does not resist the wind, nor does it cling to its petals. It simply follows its nature. If humans can learn to accept the flow, just like the flowers, the world can be a better place!

"If you tend to a flower, it will bloom, no matter how many weeds surround it." - Matshona Dhliwayo

"The present moment is filled with joy and happiness. If you are attentive, you will see it." - Thich Nhat Hanh

As highlighted, flowers are deeply connected to the five cosmic building elements of nature: Earth, Water, Air, Sunlight, and Sky. Each element plays a vital role, from subtle to coarse, in the life cycle, including ecosystems. Flowers contribute to the Earth's biodiversity forming part of the food chain and maintaining ecological balance. If nature flourishes in harmony, why do we struggle to do the same? The garden flourishes not because every flower is the same, but because each one brings something unique. What if we embraced this same truth in our communities to celebrate unity in diversity? We are all one, connected through the same breath of life, just like the flowers in the garden.

Flowers' way of life represents acceptance, freedom, peace, purity, serenity and the joy of giving. In these times of restless souls running around with anxiety and stress, while pursuing their everchanging aspirations and dreams, graceful acts of flowers may kindle the virtue of giving and sharing.

Flower the Patronus:

Throughout myths and stories, Patronus is a powerful defense that shields against Dementors - creatures that drain joy and leave only despair. In life, what if our Patronus was something as simple as a flower, radiating peace and shielding us from greed, anger, and fear so that we can be free from the Dementors of our own mind?

"Flowers whisper 'Beauty' to the world; even as they fade, wilt, and fall!" - Dr. Sun Wolf

The Valley of Flowers:

Under the stretch of the Himalayas, some places are special, enchanting, and magical. 'The Valley of Flowers' is a marvelous display of flowers. Apart from the mystery and myths of the place, with the richness of its flora and fauna, silence in the valley is a delight in solitude. In the summer months of July to October, the valley comes alive inviting the visitors for memorable experiences of one's lifetime. This UNESCO heritage site at Chamoli district, Uttarakhand in India, is the desired place to visit for many tourists.

The valley is covered with trees, flowering plants, meadows, riverbeds along with enchanting panoramic view of Himalayas. This center of plant diversity has spread of medical plants; nearly 600 species including many endangered ones. The associated story from the mythology of Lord Hanuman's life-saving herb *Sanjivini* lends credence. Animal life in the valley includes bears, reptiles, bees, butterflies, and birds of specialty.

It is popular even among tourists and five friends from Europe wanted to visit this place. Their wish was fulfilled by their visit to the valley, and they reached the planned locale with the brim of verves. The flowers spread far and wide. They went through mesmerizing waterfalls and flowing streams at a leisurely pace. They were spellbound with the beauty of the valley all the way during trekking.

"Where flowers bloom, so does hope." - Lady Bird Johnson

Amidst their joy of wandering, they noticed that they were lost in the wilderness away from the main path. Not panicking though, they were surely in a concern. They needed guidance and help from someone. Meanwhile, noticing a lonely hut down the valley, they moved towards it. Luckily, they met an old monk in white robes who appeared frail. But he was cheerful and smilingly invited them to sit on the stones outside his hut. He offered them much needed fruits and water. They relaxed and the cup of tea boosted their morale too.

Assuring them that they could reach the nearby village in two hours, the monk joined them for a long walk; a walk which turned out to be an insightful sojourn. His serene and calm demeanor had an unexplainable soothing effect on all. Their mind opened to nature's joys spontaneously.

He was conversing with them with sincere intent, pausing often. The aspects of the surroundings were engaging and educational. The flowers, streams, and sight of the heavenly landscape were relaxing.

During their walk, they came near a pond where a distinct mix of endearing aroma of flowers was felt. They paused and observed the slightly faded petals of flowers with pearly white blooms. The monk looked at them and pointed to another set of floating flowers with white and pink petals and said, "These are the legendary flowers *Bramha Kamal* and *Vishnu Kamal* which bloom only in the moonlight and represent high levels of evolved states in spiritual context."

"A flower falls, even though we love it; and a weed grows, even though we do not love it.... In this way our life should be understood. Then there is no problem." - Shunryu Suzuki

"Pure awareness is the only thing that exists - Pure, eternal and infinite." - Ramana Maharshi

He felt like spending some time in the vicinity of flowers and requested all of them to sit along the pond and pause. After some time, with all in deep thought, one of the girls Arina, an architect, broke the silence.

She shared in ecstasy, "I felt as if living within some perfect moments," she exclaimed. "I felt no past or future, but only moments here. It was relaxing and I wished it could eternally continue." She was not able to explain more and looked at the monk seeking answers.

The monk smiled and said, "It happens in a state of 'stillness' which connects us with the timeless and formless dimension within us, which is beyond thought - the pure awareness." The girl was skeptical. "I don't understand. What do you mean by pure awareness?"

He said, "All perceptions, thoughts, and feelings come and go in the light of consciousness. Pure awareness is consciousness without thoughts."

Anah, who is a businesswoman interrupted by asking, "How can we remain in the present as we always keep thinking about the past and future?" The idea of stillness sounded imaginary to her and she was a practical lady always.

She further said, "We have to learn from the past and plan for the future for a good life. It is not practical to be in the 'present' only without thoughts related to the past or future. Also, it may be possible only for people like you who live in solitude and isolation."

"A flower does not think of competing to the flower next to it. It just blooms." - Zen Shin

The monk stood up. Signaling to continue walking, he gently talked. "Surely it is difficult, but not impossible. For that, you must become a witness to thinking, in whatever activity you are in - like listening to one, looking at a person, sky, trees, and flowers. The awareness or mindfulness of the present moment will prevent you from losing yourself in thinking and external situations, whatever it may be."

For Alisa, a journalist, the issues are different. Alisa said, "Sir, we live in a world of challenges. I am a journalist, and I cover news in the most difficult situations, including the war in Ukraine. It was dark and harsh without any consideration for the value of life. I don't think it works. It may be possible for those who have nothing much to do with the world and its people."

The monk understood her predicament. He said, "These flowers have a lot to share with us about the secrets of living a beautiful life with joy, peace, and harmony even in difficult conditions." Alisa wondered and said, "They are flowers, not humans."

For Aine, who was a listener till now, it was interesting. She said, "It is good to learn from anyone and anything, particularly nature. It works. I worked as a doctor in the military and found a lot of happiness and fulfillment in treating injured soldiers despite the difficult conditions. It is like wildflowers which bloom even in extreme conditions of nature."

"Many eyes go through the meadow, but few see the flowers in it."
- Ralph Waldo Emerson

The monk said, "The Lotus flower is a good example to learn a lot. It is inspiring for wisdom and a symbol of transformation, resilience, patience, and perseverance." He stressed, "The flower is from the sludgy depths of a pond with its roots firmly anchored in the muddy depths below. But it still stands so elegant and beautiful above the water."

He continued, "The flower may grow in muddy water, but its petals remain clean and unblemished. The lotus does not fight the mud. It rises through it transforming the murkiness below into beauty above. Without struggle there is no growth. Without challenges there is no wisdom. Next time when you find your life is overwhelming, remember - if there is no mud, there is no lotus."

Aine agreed. "Yes. We have life lessons from lotus. We need to work hard despite sticking with the roots of the past and convert challenges into opportunities. We need to look up to the light with hope for new beginnings."

This impressed the monk. He said, "The lotus represents purity, poise, and enlightenment. It showcases human potential to overcome suffering. These traits are helpful to grow, develop, and transform. We can evolve as good humans with love and compassion for all. The lotus is not affected by the pollution of murky waters. Besides, it even purifies the water it grows in."

Ananya, a management consultant, was enthused to share her view. For her, the interconnection of petals was a

---

"Don't wait for someone to bring you flowers. Plant your own garden and decorate your own soul." - Luther Burbank

"Flowers don't tell, they show." - Stephanie Skeem

revelation. She said, "These petals embody the principle of interdependence in the web of existence."

Another of her observations was equally mature. "The blossom and eventual fading of flowers is symbolic of the impermanence in nature."

Arina felt that the lessons from the 'Valley of Flowers' are illuminating. Holding and savoring the fragrance of a few jasmine flowers, she teased the monk, "What is the spiritual message from jasmine flowers?"

The monk, in his smiles as always, briefed her. "The fragrance of the white jasmine indicates virtuous qualities and the wholesome actions of a pure heart; note its white hues. It is associated with simplicity, humility, and contentment."

They were nearing the village. At first, they only wanted help and guidance to reach the tourist point but as they walked, they realized and discovered something deeper - clarity, presence, and peace they hadn't felt before.

Arina wanted to know from the monk the comprehensive message from the 'Valley of Flowers' before parting and asked him, "If a valley flourishes because of its many different flowers, can we not do the same as people? What if we embrace our diversity as something to celebrate, rather than divide us?"

The monk agreed and said, "Yes. We don't have to compete with each other but work together to live in peace, accepting our diversity and celebrating unity. Though the

---

"How do I become still? By flowing with the stream." - Lao Tzu

forms are many, the essence is one. The diversity of life is not something to fear or divide us; it is the beauty of creation with each form an expression of the same energy."

The monk concluded, "Through the 'Valley of Flowers', all of you are witnessing Buddha's way and his noble eightfold path. The noble eightfold path is the inward journey to beckon the dormant wisdom in us already. It is not to take us somewhere but to come back to freedom of wisdom which is always there right here within all of us."

The monk's pearl of wisdom outlined:

True happiness trails the pure heart and the mind like a shadow. If we can flower the way of our life, the light of one's inner peace shall kindle many lamps.

We can be the best version of ourselves: loving, kind, joyful, gentle, giving, and caring with gratitude for nature's blessings. That is our potential.

To live like a flower is to give without expectation, to stand with grace, and to cause no harm. This is the way of nature! This is the way of peace!!

Imagine living one day as mindfully as a flower exists, fully present and freely offering beauty and harmony. How might that shift your relationships, your community, or your world?

"The very best relationship has a gardener and a flower. The gardener nurtures and the flower blooms." - Carole Radziwill

References

1. Ramana Maharshi, (2015), ***Who am I?***, Open Sky Press Limited

2. William Hart, (1987), ***The Art of Living: Vipassana Meditation as Taught by S.N. Goenka***, Harper & Row

3. Paramahansa Yogananda, (1946), ***Autobiography of a Yogi***, Yogoda Satsanga Society of India

4. Swami Ranganathananda, (1958), ***Eternal values for a changing society***, Advaita Ashrama

5. Swami Vivekananda, (2016), ***The Complete Works of Swami Vivekananda***, Advaita Ashrama

6. Stephen Hawking, (2001), ***The Universe in a Nutshell***, Random House Publishing Group

7. Gary Zukav, (1979), ***The Dancing Wu Li Masters***, William Morrow

8. Stephen Hawking, (2002), ***The Theory of Everything: The Origin and Fate of the Universe***, Jaico Publishing House

9. Stephen Hawking, (1988), ***A Brief History of Time***, Bantam Dell Publishing Group

10. Eknath Easwaran, (2020), ***The Bhagavad Gita for Daily Living,*** Nilgiri Press

11. Eknath Easwaran, (1981), ***Essence of the Upanishads***, Nilgiri Press

12. Eckhart Tolle, (1997), ***The Power of Now: A Guide to Spiritual Enlightenment***, Namaste Pub

13. Eckhart Tolle, (2003), ***Stillness Speaks***, New World Library

14. Eckhart Tolle, (2008), ***Oneness with All Life: Inspirational Selections from A New Earth***, Penguin Publishing Group

15. Thich Nhat Hanh, (1997), ***The Heart of the Buddha's Teaching: Transforming Suffering into Peace***, Joy and Liberation, Parallax Press

16. Yuval Noah Harari, (2011), ***Sapiens: A Brief History of Humankind***, Dvir Publishing House Ltd.

17. Fritjof Capra, (1975), ***The Tao of Physics***, Shambhala Publications

18. Richard P. Feynman, (1999), ***The Pleasure of Finding Things Out***, Perseus Books (USA)

19. Bhikkhu Bodhi, (1995), ***The Middle Length Discourses of the Buddha: A Translation of the Majjhima Nikaya***, Wisdom Publications

20. Sumedho Thera, (1995), ***The Long Discourses of the Buddha: A Translation of the Digha Nikaya***, Wisdom Publications

21. Desmond Biddulph, Darcy Flynn, (1993), ***Teachings of the Buddha: The Wisdom of the Dharma, from the Pali Canon to the Sutras***, Thorsons

22. Gavin Harrison, (2003), ***In the Lap of the Buddha***, Shambhala Publications

23. H.H. the Fourteenth Dalai Lama, Tenzin Gyatso, (2001), ***Kindness, Clarity, and Insight***, Snow Lion Publications

24. Swami Rama Tirtha, (1910), ***In the Woods of God - Realization***, Ramakrishna-Vivekananda Center

25. Venerable Ledi Sayadaw, (1969), ***The Manuals of Dhamma***, The Buddhist Publication Society

26. Buddha, (1998), ***Mahasatipatthana Sutta***, Vipassana Research Institute

27. Bhadantacariya Buddhaghosa, translated by Bhikkhu Nanamoli, (1956), ***The Visuddhimagga The Path of Purification***, Buddhist Publication Society

28. K. Sri Dhammananda, (1987), ***The Dhammapada***, The Buddhist Missionary Society

29. Bhikkhu Bodhi, (1993), ***A Comprehensive Manual of Abhidhamma***, The Buddhist Publication Society

30. Paul R. Fleischman, M.D, (1993), ***An Ancient Path: Introductory Talk on Vipassana Meditation as Taught by S. N. Goenka***, The Vipassana Research Institute

31. Ambale Naga, (2015), ***Basavanna: A Phenomenon: Beyond Boundaries and Times: Social and Spiritual Reformer***, Notion Press

32. Hermann Hesse, (1922), ***Siddhartha***, S. Fischer Verlag